庄子

ZHUANGZI

(c.369 BC-286 BC)

The Wisdom of China

ZHUANGZI

Enjoyment of Life in an Untroubled State

By Xu Yuanxiang & Yin Yongjian

CHINA INTERCONTINENTAL PRESS

CONTENTS

自煎桂可食故伐之漆可用故割之世皆知有

用之用不知無用之用也

莊子內篇第六 大宗師

古之真人其寢不夢 注云無意想也 其覺無憂 注云當所遇而安也

泉涸魚相與處於陸相呴以濕相濡以沫不相忘於江湖

夫大塊載我以形勞我以生佚我以老息我以死也 藏舟於壑

藏山於澤夜半有力者而走昧者不知 注云方

Preface

In the Christian *Bible*, angels with wings on their shoulders act as God's assistants; the Chinese often picture such romantic imagery as a kind of butterfly, a kind of beautiful insect.

One day more than 2,300 years ago, a young man named Zhuang Zhou dreamed of a butterfly. In the dream, he travelled in a leisurely manner and in the end confused his own identity with that of the butterfly, so much so that when he woke he thought he was still the butterfly. "Zhuang Zhou Dreaming of a Butterfly" is the earliest story involving humans and butterflies in China.

Perhaps it was this dream that activated a new philosophical direction - a

Angel in *The Sistine Madonna* by Raffaello Sanzio.

transcendence of the secular world which added invisible wings to imagination, so as to make it "fly" higher and wider. Since that time, another high point was reached in the history of Chinese philosophy and thought.

That high point was the life and work of Zhuangzi, a giant of Taoism who followed Lao Tzu. Just as Confucianism is inseparable from the doctrines of Confucius and Mencius, so too Lao Tzu

Zhuang Zhou's Dreaming of Becoming a Butterfly.

and Zhuangzi embody the very essence of Taoism in China. If Lao Tzu is the founder and ultimate source of Taoism, Zhuangzi is a key thinker who carried forward a local philosophy of religion, and formed a unique and powerful system of thought, which retains its considerable power today in the modern world.

翦桂可食故伐之漆可用故割之皆知有

用之用不知無用之用也

莊子內篇第六大宗師

古之真人其寢不夢郭云無意想也其覺無憂注云當所遇而安也泉

涸魚相與處於陸相呴以濕相濡以沫不相忘於江湖

大塊載我以形勞我以生以老息我以死也藏舟於壑

山於澤夜半有力者而走昧者不知注云

Zhuangzi's Birth and Death

Around the 5th century BC, there occurred an extremely important civilizational period in human history. That era produced many of the greatest philosophers that humanity has ever produced including: Socrates, Democritus, and Aristotle from western countries; Sakyamuni of India; and the great founders

Statue of Socrates (469 BC-399 BC).

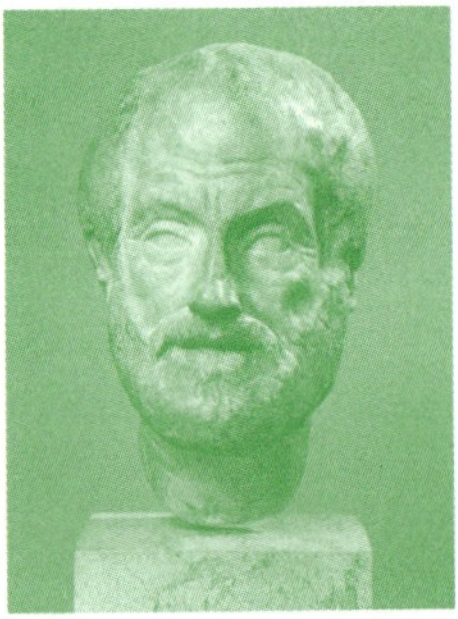

Statue of Aristotle (384 BC-322 BC).

Portrait of Confucius.

Portrait of Lao Tzu.

of Oriental culture - Lao Tzu, Confucius and Mo Tzu.

While the Greek philosophers thought about the relationship between man and the things around him, Indian philosophers were pondering the relationship between man and God, and Chinese philosophers were concerning themselves with the intricacies of human relations. In such an unprecedented era of blossoming philosophy and thought, Zhuangzi, the miraculous dreamer, made his appearance in ancient China.

However, what Zhuangzi thought about was not limited to interpersonal relationships, but rather extended beyond the limitations of any knowledge hierarchy and ideology. He thought deeply about life from the perspectives of "natural law" and social problems. He regarded the absolute freedom of the human spirit as the highest pursuit of life. His philosophy is a kind of life philosophy. More importantly, his doctrine covers all aspects of social life.

In the numerous books and records about ancient China, no details of Zhuangzi's birth and death can be found. The dates of his birth and death were a source of debate for later generations who sought to link his activities and thought with a biography with clearly defined bookends. Nowadays, most people go along with the conclusion reached by Qian Mu, a famous Chinese scholar from the early 20th century. In his book *Chronological Studies of the Pre-Qin Philosophers* (published in 1935), Qian reckoned that Zhuangzi was born between 368 BC and 359 BC, and died between 289 BC and 279 BC.

Chronological Studies of the Pre-Qin Philosophers.

Zhuangzi lived in the Warring States Period, a time full of blood and gunpowder smoke. In his writing, he describes many characters with physical disabilities, and even recorded his dialogues with skeletons he encountered in the wilderness. Such maimed bodies and skeletons which littered the mountains and plains give a taste of what life must have been like in this barbaric and cruel era.

The Warring States Period was a time of bloody battles.

Why did Zhuangzi pursue spiritual freedom in such a turbulent social environment? What made him have such an incongruously crazy and fantastical dream?

When communicating his ideas, Zhuangzi often imitated the speaking manner of Confucius, the founder of Confucianism. It can be seen from this that Confucianism had become the mainstream ideology at that time. All states held aloft, at least nominally, the banners of "benevolence, justice, propriety and wisdom" to attract ruling elites. Like Confucius, the vast majority of scholars desired to have official careers.

In such an era where men of talent were in such urgent demand, Zhuangzi chose a different way of life. As recorded in the *Records of the Historian* written by the famous historian Sima Qian of the Han Dynasty, Zhuangzi only served as an

Portrait of Sima Qian.

official once in his lifetime. His official position was that of Qiyuanli, similar to what is today a kind of Park Administrator. As a person of low social class, he spent most of his lifetime mired in poverty.

How could such a poverty-stricken person construct a philosophical and spiritual paradise while all the time resisting the temptations of fame and fortune and advancement?

Zhuangzi lived in the State of Song, which was located near the borders of what is today Henan, Shandong and Anhui provinces. He was born in a place called Meng. Now it is impossible to determine the specific location of Meng. The controversy about his hometown has raged for more than 2,000 years.

There are three schools of thought concerning the location of Zhuangzi's hometown: some say it is today's Shangqiu County in Henan Province; some say Caoxian County in Shandong; while others maintain that Mengcheng in Anhui is the true hometown of Zhuangzi. Academic opinion tends to believe that Caoxian County and Shangqiu County are basically one and the same place. So, the controversy tends to focus on Shangqiu and Mengcheng nowadays. Both Shangqiu and Mengcheng insist that they are the hometown of Zhuangzi. Historians are more likely to favor Shangqiu because Sima Qian said in the *Records of the Historian* that Zhuangzi was born in Meng. In the era of Zhuangzi, the State of Song had a place called Meng which is near Shangqiu in Henan. However, no record of today's Mengcheng in Anhui can be found in the literary records dating back more than 2,300 years.

Historical research shows that Minquan County in the northwest of Shangqiu City in Henan Province, is an area which was home to many people with the surname "Zhuang". In recent years, Minquan has attracted people from around the world with the surname "Zhuang". They go to Minquan to seek their roots and worship their ancestors. They all find time to visit a place called the Qinglian Temple because it is reputed to be the legendary hometown of Zhuangzi.

Compared to the famous and magnificent Confucian Mansion, Temple and Cemetery complex in Qufu in Shandong, the hometown of Confucius, the hometown of Zhuangzi seems very paltry – it seems just like any ordinary village in China. Green trees and red walls, crowing cocks and

Zhuangzi's hometown – Qingliansi Village, Minquan County, Henan Province.

Ancestor Worship Ceremony: Offspring of Zhuangzi attended the Fifth China Minquan International Zhuangzi Cultural Festival in October 2012.

barking dogs backdrop a peaceful pastoral scene. The living environments and legacies of the Confucian and Taoist sages seem quite different: Confucian representatives such as Confucius and Mencius advocated the idea of going into society and these ideas found respect and favor with many ancient emperors and officials, and thus have been, and are today, widely revered by generations of people. The Taoist master Zhuangzi put forward the idea of desocialization – of secluding oneself in a quiet and isolated place in the countryside. But his life philosophy of remaining indifferent and inactive has had a profound if somewhat less conscious influence on people.

It is said that the former residence of Zhuangzi is located in an alley in the north of the village. South of the former residence is the Zhuangzi School, where Zhuangzi taught his disciples. The alley was named "Zhuangzi Alley" in later years. But due to the continuous chaos caused by war and flooding, the Zhuangzi Alley and its subsidiary buildings have all disappeared.

This alley was more than 120 meters long. Its northernmost end was the site of Zhuangzi's former residence, and south of the alley was the site of the Zhuangzi School. Both sites were inundated by

Archway of the Zhuangzi Cemetery in Minquan.

flooding in later years. But in order to commemorate the life and work of Zhuangzi, the area was kept free of any housing or buildings for many years. The sites have remained. Some local elderly people recall a well-known legend: On some nights when the breeze blows and there is a bright moon, a mirage often appears in the Zhuangzi Alley, and people are granted a vision of the former residence of Zhuangzi.

There is an old well in this alley. According to legend, it was dug by Zhuangzi, but was repeatedly flooded by the overflowing waters of the Yellow River in later years. After numerous renovations, it remains there today. This well is called "Zhuangzi Well" by the locals.

In the 18th century, the scholar Zhang Liangke wrote a famous poem beside the Zhuangzi Well: "The garden of the sage Zhuangzi is so wonderful in the sunset, with his fragrant spring well. Residents have no need to sigh because the Zhuangzi Well still gives water". It is said that the well was more than 10 meters deep at that time, with black and shiny walls, and offering clear and sweet water.

Zhuangzi Well.

Time has changed the former residence of Zhuangzi into a heap of loess now and has driven away most remaining folk memories. Apart from the Zhuangzi Well which the locals cherish very much, no trace of Zhuangzi can be found....

自煎桂可食故伐之漆可用故割之皆知有
用之用不知無用之用也
莊子內篇第六 大宗師
之真人其寢不夢 注云無意想也 其覺無憂 注云當所遇而安也 泉
涸魚相與處於陸相呴以溼相濡以沫不如相忘於江湖
大塊載我以形勞我以生佚我以老息我已死也 藏舟於壑
山於澤夜半有力者而負之走昧者不知 注云方

'Tao Te Ching' and 'Nan Hua Jing'

Zhuangzi once made a long journey when he was young. It is said that his decision to travel was made because of his reading of the *Tao Te Ching*, a small book that was not at all famous at that time. Despite its relatively few words, this small book brought home to Zhuangzi a principle which would guide his whole life: The Tao (Way) follows nature.

Tao Te Ching.

The *Tao Te Ching* was written by Li Er, namely

Portrait of Lao Tzu.

Lao Tzu, the founder of Taoism in China. In this book consisting of no more than 5,000 characters, Lao Tzu discussed an eternal topic, namely the relationship between man and the universe. He came to the conclusion that man must respect the laws of nature, must maintain nature in its original form, and must always seek to be quiet and inactive.

Lao Tzu pointed out that the human spirit should return as much as possible to the original state of the baby.

In the social environment at that time where people were ardently pursuing fame and fortune, Lao Tzu's viewpoint seemed a very sedate and counter-intuitive philosophy. It gave Zhuangzi a glimpse of new values which lay beyond secular ideas and afforded him a criterion whereby he could judge right from wrong from the perspective of nature.

Orthodox Confucianism always analyzes civilization and sees its positive aspects. But Zhuangzi thought civilization had much about it that was negative.

Zhuangzi gave an example: In the past, horses were free to eat grass, drink water and roam on the grasslands. But Bo Le (an ancient figure famed for his horsemanship) imposed horseshoes and saddles on these beasts. To make them run faster, Bo Le hit them with a whip. As a result, many horses died. Zhuangzi thought such behavior restrained the horse's true nature – its free-running wildness.

Through the example of Bo Le, Zhuangzi expressed his contrary attitude towards

Zhuangzi believed that the horses should be free to gallop in the grasslands.

civilization.

How could the true meaning of civilization be explored?

To trace the most elemental human nature, Zhuangzi left home and headed for the south of the Chu State. Formerly called the "Land of the Barbarians" by the people in the Central Plains, it is located along the shores of what is Dongting Lake today. Here

Dongting Lake.

there are beautiful landscapes and simple and honest people. Due to the remoteness of this place, almost no trace of the rituals and music culture which prevailed in the Central Plains could be found here.

Local people maintained a primitive lifestyle and followed age-old customs which had almost no place for etiquette and cultivation. The people in the Central Plains believed in the dragon culture, while local people worshipped a kind of legendary sacred bird called the phoenix. The phoenixes which were engraved on local utensils always raised their wings and heads high. The people believed themselves to be the descendants of the Sun God and Fire God, so in general they preferred bright strong colors. They were enthusiastic and unrestrained like fire. These characteristics are reflected in their colorful costumes and unique sacrificial ceremonies.

Zhuangzi witnessed one of these unforgettable ritual ceremonies. A good-looking and coquettish witch dressing up like a human and lured a wizard dressed up as a god. The bold and unrestrained love between human being and God was portrayed on the stage. They sang and danced in the open field, and fully enjoyed themselves. Such noisy and joyous scenes were so much different from the dignified sacrificial rituals of the Central Plains.

Zhuangzi experienced a return of an elemental human nature in a place far from his hometown. The simple, unrestrained and straightforward personalities of the local people brought him back to the most elemental, natural and real of human emotions.

There are no more details about this trip

Zhuangzi witnessed the ritual ceremony.

taken by Zhuangzi,. However, the impact of this tour on his life is indisputable. Along with the profound introspection it inspired in him regarding the essence of human nature, Zhuangzi started to look with new insight at the devastation of the world and the restlessness of society.

If a civilization is so developed that most people come to regard it as the standard, any person violating that standard will be excluded by the society because people generally regard him or her as aberrant in

Taoist paper-cut: *Eight Immortals Crossing the Surging Sea.*

their thinking.

In an era where Confucianism played the dominant role, Zhuangzi taught that in fact, people can choose a different path of life. One civilization imposed on all people restricts the essence of human nature.

One famous saying attributed to Zhuangzi is: "Gentlemen of ancient China believed in feudal ethics and rites, but were very pedantic and hypocritical." That is to say, the originally free, and varied heart is possibly constrained by adhering to just one standard.

煎桂可食故伐之漆可用故割之皆知有

用之用不知無用之用也

莊子內篇第六 大宗師

之真人其寢不夢 注云無意想也 其覺無憂 注云當所遇而安也

魚相與處於陸相呴以濕相濡以沫不相忘於江湖

大塊載我以形勞我以生以老息我已死也 藏舟於壑

山於澤夜半有力者負之而走昧者不知 注云

Cross-Cultural Echoes: Zhuangzi and Spinoza

In the 1650s, a Jew in a remote village south of Amsterdam, began to write his most important book *Ethics*. Some years before, he had been excluded from the local Jewish synagogue, and was expelled from the Jewish quarter. He had been forced into a life of seclusion.

This person was Spinoza, the famous Dutch philosopher.

Benedictus Spinoza (1632-1677).

Spinoza was born into a rich family, but from the start was somewhat of a black sheep unlike his peers. How did he make a living after leaving home? In the end, he found a job grinding optical lenses. He could never imagine that a Chinese philosopher who lived more than 2,000 years ago had had a very similar experience. The Chinese philosopher had chosen an even lower and more inconspicuous profession - that of making straw sandals!

Photos on *Ethics*.

This philosopher was Zhuangzi.

Zhuangzi lived in much greater poverty than Spinoza, and he often suffered from hunger. Especially after he gave up his post as Qiyuanli, he often had literally nothing to eat.

One time when he had run out of grain,

Portrait of Zhuangzi.

a frustrated Zhuangzi thought of Jianhehou, the local official in charge of water conservancy. It is said that Zhuangzi had had a lot of contact with Jianhehou during the period when he served as Qiyuanli. Jianhehou was relatively well off. Therefore, Zhuangzi hoped to ask for some emergency food. Zhuangzi dressed in rags and walked to the front gate of Jianhehou's mansion.

Jianhehou said: "No problem! I can lend you 300 taels of gold when my salary is paid in the autumn."

Realizing Jianhehou was unwilling to give him any food, Zhuangzi was very angry because his family faced starvation. He said: "Jianhehou, you liked listening to my fables so much in the past. Now, I'll tell you another story."

Jianhehou said: "Please do!"

Zhuangzi said: "I heard someone say 'Mr. Zhuang' on the way to your mansion. I looked back but saw nobody. Finally I found a little carp in the gutter. The little carp said: 'I am an official of the Dragon King of the East Sea. I am here for the huge rain and wind. If you can provide me with a bucket of water, I will be able to survive.' Zhuangzi said: 'Soon, I will go to the Wu State and the Yue State. I can release you into the waters of the Xijiang River.' The carp said: 'Alas! Such aid is too slow to be helpful. I will have died before then. Tomorrow, you will find me in the dried fish market'."

After telling the story, Zhuangzi left Jianhehou's mansion with nothing. It is said that from that day, Zhuangzi chose to follow

Zhuangzi found a little carp in the gutter, and promised to release it into a river later. The fish replied that it would be too late to do that. "Tomorrow, you will find me in the dried fish market," it said.

an ignoble career path to feed himself and his family . He gathered up a kind of local plant named gecao. He used the leaves to weave straw sandals and he sold them to passers by.

自煎桂可食故伐之漆可用故割之人皆知有

用之用不知無用之用也

莊子內篇第六 大宗師

古之真人其寢不夢 郭云無意想也 其覺無憂 注云當所遇而安也 泉

涸魚相與處於陸相呴以濕相濡以沫不相忘於江湖

夫大塊載我以形勞我以生人老息我以死也藏舟於壑

藏山於澤夜半有力者而走昧者不知 注云 [illegible]

Founder of Chinese Life Philosophy

Zhuangzi recorded many of his life experiences in a book *Nan Hua Jing*, also known as *Zhuangzi*. Through the ages, the *Nan Hua Jing* has been regarded as a "classic of wisdom" by generations of Chinese people and has become the main source for later generations seeking to

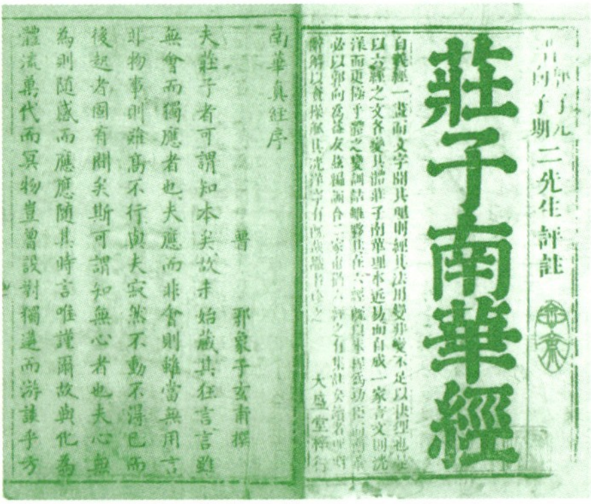

Nan Hua Jing by Zhuangzi.

understand the life and thought of Zhuangzi.

Portrait of Jin Shengtan (1608-1660).

A famous critic called Jin Shengtan in the 17th century produced annotated commentaries on the works of six major ancient Chinese thinkers, including the *Zhuangzi*.

The earliest mention of the *Zhuangzi* can be found in *Hanshu Yiwenzhi* (bibliographical section of the *History of the Former Han Dynasty*). *Hanshu Yiwenzhi* mainly categorizes books handed down from the pre-Qin period, and classifies the volumes into ten major categories, i.e., Confucianism, Legalism, the School of Logicians, Mohism, Taoism, the Yin-Yang School, and the School of Diplomacy, and others. The *Zhuangzi* was classified under Taoism. The *Zhuangzi* as annotated in the *Hanshu Yiwenzhi* consists of 52 chapters. Today's *Zhuangzi* comes from the annotated version by Guo Xiang in the Wei and Jin Dynasties. It comprises 33 chapters, including 7 inner chapters, 15 outer chapters and 11 miscellaneous chapters.

People generally think the inner chapters were written by Zhuangzi, while other parts were written by his disciples or scholars of an earlier age. The *Zhuangzi* is regarded as the work of the Zhuangzi School.

In February 724, Emperor Li Longji of the Tang Dynasty issued an imperial decree, and conferred the title "Nanhua Immortal" on Zhuangzi, making him the first of four major immortals of Taoism, the local Chinese religion. The so-called "Immortal" became a personage to be worshiped and imitated by Taoist disciples. Since then, the *Zhuangzi* had become one of the four classics of Taoism.

Li Longji (Tang Emperor Xuanzong, 685-762).

Zhuangzi in the *Nan Hua Jing* is a humorous master very adept at telling stories. Humorous fables are the writer's primary means of expressing his ideas. Through poetic language, he depicts the ideal realm of freedom and romance which goes beyond money and status. Zhuangzi suffered great poverty so it is an interesting question to ask: What was Zhuangzi's attitude towards poverty?

The king of a neighboring state wanted to meet the "immortal" Zhuangzi after hearing about his talent. But to the surprise of the king, Zhuangzi appeared in rags, wearing clothing full of patches. His shoes were tied with straw rope rather than with laces.

The king asked Zhuangzi: "Why do you

Portrait of Zhuangzi, the"Nanhua Immortal".

look so tired and bedraggled?"

Zhuangzi answered: "This is poverty not tiredness. Scholars with integrity feel tired when they cannot realize their ideals. I was born at the wrong time. I am so poor because of the constant wars between states."

Zhuangzi thought that an individual cannot completely grasp his/her fate. We come into a world with an existing situation, and we have to accept many established conditions in order to survive. But our hearts are clever and free, and we can reach a very high realm.

Although Zhuangzi was very poor, he described an extremely beautiful realm of "Enjoyment of Life in an Untroubled State", which has influenced Chinese for more than 2,000 years.

Zhuangzi admitted his material poverty openly, but he firmly denied any spiritual

Zhuangzi went to see the king of the Wei in shabby dress.

decadence. This is Zhuangzi's attitude towards poverty. He thought spiritual poverty much worse than material poverty. Zhuangzi was poor in life but rich in spirit.

Photo on *Zhuangzi*.

Sometimes poverty makes people completely frustrated, and sometimes it makes people give much more attention to fame and fortune.

Fortune represents money and wealth. Since ancient times, there has been a famous saying in China: People come together or separate because of money.

What was Zhuangzi's attitude towards money and fortune?

One day, Cao Shang, with a retinue of hundreds of horses and carriages, came to

Zhuangzi's home to show off his fortune which he hoped would offer a withering contrast to of Zhuangzi's straitened existence.

Cao Shang said to Zhuangzi: "If I lived in such a hovel in such a shabby alley, and made my living by weaving straw sandals, I am afraid I would rather choose death. Do you know who I am? I have the ear of a king of a strong state who offers me wealth and hundreds of horses and carriages. This is who I am."

As an envoy of the Song State, Cao Shang had gone to the Qin State, a strong state in the western part of ancient China. The king of the Song State presented him with a number of horses and carriages before he left. After reaching the Qin State, Cao Shang won the favor of the king of Qin because of shameless flattery. When he left the Qin State, the king of Qin awarded

Cultural Center in Minquan, hometown of Zhuangzi.

him hundreds of horses and carriages. Cao Shang regarded this as a great achievement. So that is how he came to appear so very confident and proud in front of Zhuangzi.

Zhuangzi answered: "Suppose the king of Qin is ill. Anyone who can cure the king's abscess would get one carriage, and anyone who could lick his hemorrhoid could get five carriages. I really am very interested to know how you came to get 100 carriages!"

Zhuangzi thought that if a person lost

sight of his true nature and pursued fortune without scruple, he would become the slave of money. Such people he saw as being the most pitiful. This was Zhuangzi's attitude towards money and fortune.

Many Chinese people with lofty ideals perhaps can resist the temptations of money but fame can be a very strong temptress.

Fame represents the status and honor that people enjoy in the eyes of others. As a Chinese saying goes: A man leaves his name behind wherever he stays, just as a goose leaves the echo of its cry wherever it flies. What was Zhuangzi's attitude towards fame?

Zhuangzi had a very good friend who was his lifelong study partner. Like Zhuangzi, he was also a very famous scholar, but his status was much higher than that of Zhuangzi. He was Hui Shi who had served as the Prime Minister of the Wei State.

Kaifeng, which was less than 100 km away from Zhuangzi's hometown, was the capital of the Wei State during the Warring States Period. At that time, Kaifeng was called "Daliang". One day 2,300 years ago, Prime Minister Hui Shi heard that his classmate and friend Zhuangzi had arrived in the Wei State to meet with him.

At that moment, someone tried to incite disharmony between them: "Zhuangzi will replace you as prime minister because his

Landscape in Kaifeng, Henan Province.

Zhuangzi told Hui Shi a story about the holy and pure bird in the south.

writing style and eloquence are greater than yours."

Although Hui Shi did not fully believe this report, he did worry that he would be replaced because he knew well the talent and the wisdom of Zhuangzi. Therefore, he ordered that Zhuangzi be arrested in Daliang.

However, Zhuangzi suddenly appeared in front of him several days later. Zhuangzi told Hui Shi a story about birds: "There is a kind of holy and pure bird in the south. They perch only on the phoenix tree, eat only the fruit of the bamboo, and drink only the sweetest of spring water. However, the owls often yell to scare such birds to prevent them from chasing maggoty rats. Do you want to frighten me by mobilizing so many people to find me?"

In the eyes of Zhuangzi, an official title was nothing but a maggoty rat. This was

Zhuangzi's attitude towards honor and status.

Zhuangzi did not believe in one of the central ideas advocated by Confucianism - that a man can obtain dignity from power in an open and above-board way.

The story about Zhuangzi and Hui Shi, expressed his understanding of power to a large extent, and his inherent distrust of power. He thought that power was a kind of negative, destructive and oppressive force. He pursued freedom and the leisure to do as he pleased and go where he pleased. But in a society dominated by power, he was restrained and could not live freely.

In 1673, Spinoza was expelled from the Jewish quarter and banished for 17 years. He was just about to finish his book *Ethics* when he finally was offered another job opportunity. Someone offered him a job teaching in the Philosophy Department of

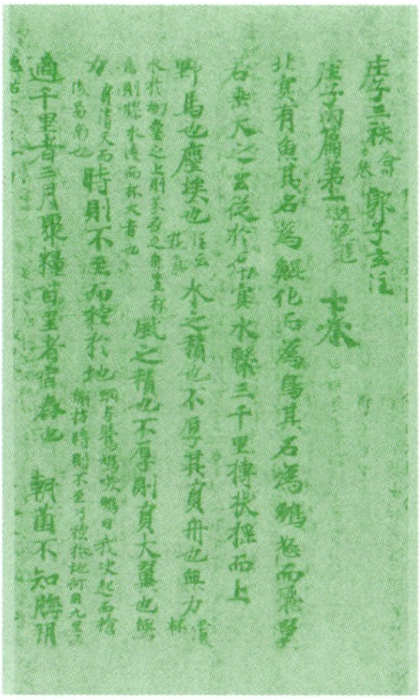

Photo about *Zhuangzi: Inner Chapters.*

Heidelberg University, but it came with the proviso that he could not make any comments relating to religion.

Spinoza refused the offer politely. Approximately 2,000 years ago, Zhuangzi had turned down a similarly potentially life-changing opportunity without a second thought.

Zhuangzi lived in a place cut by two

rivers, namely the Pushui River and the Haoshui River. Many of the stories about his life are related to these two rivers.

Zhuangzi liked fishing. One time when he was fishing along the Pushui River, two people came from a distant place. They stood behind him and said very respectfully: "Our king has invited you to be his prime minister!"

The two people were messengers from the Chu State. They had been entrusted by the king of Chu to invite Zhuangzi to be their prime minister. This kind of official position was what many scholars spent their lives yearning for. The Chu State was a place where Zhuangzi had longed to go. Such a prominent position would transform his poor and lowly life. Nevertheless, how did Zhuangzi treat this sudden opportunity for advancement and glory?

He even did not look around. Still

The king of the Chu State sent envoys to invite Zhuangzi to be his prime minister, but Zhangzi refused in a clever way.

grasping his fishing rod, he said: "I heard your turtle god has been dead for 3,000 years. The dead turtle wrapped in a bamboo box has been enshrined and is worshiped in the temple. Do you think the turtle would prefer to crawl around in the mud or be worshiped by people?"

The two messengers replied: "Crawl in the mud, of course."

Zhuangzi said: "That is true and now, you can leave. I prefer to be the live turtle."

Regarding such tales of the life of Zhuangzi, Sima Qian gives us a different version of the story in his book *Records of the Historian*. But in the story, Zhuangzi was also unwilling to become an official. The king of the Chu State invited him to be prime minister. Despite a number of lavish gifts, he refused the invitation. He said that he preferred to be a calf in the countryside.

Zhuangzi thought that taking an official post would harm his essential human nature, and he preferred to enjoy his freedom despite his poverty and low status. He thought only freedom and life had any value, and he thought nothing of dazzling honor and noble status. Zhuangzi would always choose the ordinary life rather than a glorious death. This was his philosophy of life.

自煎桂可食故伐之漆可用故割之皆知有
用之用不知無用之用也

莊子內篇第六 大宗師

古之真人其寢不夢 郭云無意想也 其覺無憂 郭云當所遇而安也 泉
涸魚相与處於陸相呴以濕相濡以沫不相忘於江湖
夫大塊載我以形勞我以生佚以老息我已死也 藏舟於壑
藏山於澤夜半有力者而走昧者不知注云

The Separation of Taoism and Confucianism

Almost at the same time as Zhuangzi lived, there was another great thinker who expressed a quite different idea on life: "Sacrifice one's life for a righteous cause". In other words, life can be sacrificed ~~to~~ to serve a great truth. This man was Mencius, one of the giants of Confucianism.

The life philosophy of Zhuangzi is very different from that of Mencius. Mencius stressed moral undertakings, namely that "God would give an important task to a certain person."

Portrait of Mencius.

Confucianism placed more emphasis on fame and moral undertakings. However, Zhuangzi believed that achievements are conditional, while people can control themselves in pursuit of freedom, especially spiritual freedom.

Benevolence and justice are the symbols of Confucianism; the way and morality are the essence of Taoism. Confucianism emphasizes artificial constraints; Taoism focuses more on nature. In terms of life

Mencius Temple in Zoucheng, Shandong Province.

philosophy, Confucianism emphasizes indoctrination, education and persuasion, while Taoism stresses abandonment and forgetting, and keeping quiet.

Zhuangzi summarized nature as "natural law", and called behavior that satisfied natural law "morality". He thought that all "artificial" factors deviate from nature. The compound word "Ren Wei (in Chinese)" includes the character "Wei", which means "false". So Zhuangzi advocated abandoning the false parts of human nature. He thought that real life was natural. All artificial education and persuasion lost all significance in the face of this truth, and so should be abandoned.

So Zhuangzi taught us to give up things sometimes.

It is said that there is a sign along an Alpine path that reads: Go slowly and enjoy yourself!

The Taoist Holy Land - Gansu Kongtong Mountain in Pingliang.

Similarly, Zhuangzi suggested that people learn to appreciate. During the course of one's life, one should appreciate instead of forging ahead blindly. To a certain extent, people should learn to exit, but this does not mean any abandonment of exertion, struggle or pursuit. Seen from the outside, it is a kind of negative behavior. But in fact, it is a return to nature. In this way, more opportunities may become available.

To vividly explain "nature", Zhuangzi told a fable about how "Hun Dun died after his Qiqiao was opened" at the end of his seventh article.

Qiqiao refers to the five sense organs. As a man without the five sense organs, Hun Dun was isolated from the outside world. Hun Dun was a figure made up by Zhuangzi. Hun Dun represents the most original and pure natural living state.

Hun Dun was an emperor of the Central

The destruction of the natural nature yields disastrous result.

Plains. One day, the emperors of the South and North Seas visited him. He treated them with the utmost cordiality. To thank their kind and passionate host, the two emperors decided to open up the five sense organs of Hun Dun to allow him to experience the world like a normal person.

Thus, the two emperors opened one aperture for him every day. On the seventh day, all seven apertures were opened.

Dacheng Hall of the Confucian Temple.

But when Hun Dun began to experience the world, he lost himself. The artificial opening eventually ruined his natural instincts. Hun Dun died.

Traditional Confucianism believes that saints have established systems and standards for us, showing us the right and appropriate way to live.

Zhuangzi came to realize the opposite. Everything has two sides, namely the positive and the negative. If we remove two sides, the status of Hun Dun, the Tao (way), completeness and original simplicity will be achieved.

Zhuangzi often mentioned Confucius in his articles. Unlike Lao Tzu, the founder of Taoism, Confucius appears frequently in Zhuangzi's articles. However, Confucius always plays an old-fashioned negative role, and Zhuangzi always criticizes him. In his book, Zhuangzi always reprimands

Confucius using aggressive words.

On the whole, Zhuangzi tried to speak against and offer alternatives to some Confucian values throughout his life. He worked tirelessly to reveal the possible negative elements hidden behind Confucian thought. For example, the Confucian School highly praised order in society, but representatives of the Taoist School such as Zhuangzi believed that order may be lost and damaged. In the case of damage, it would result in chaos. So it is better to return to the original state of nature instead of order.

Like Confucius, Zhuangzi also visited many states. But Confucius did so to lobby kings and realize his ideal of "benevolent rule through adherence to ritual". Zhuangzi did so to inspire kings to return to nature.

In a space of less than 200 years, Confucius and Zhuangzi both went to Qufu in Shandong, the hometown of Confucius - a land of "etiquette".

Qufu was the capital of the Lu State at that time. One day, a foreign mission arrived. It is said there was one person in the mission who wanted to persuade the king to abdicate. This person was Zhuangzi.

In Qufu, the cradle of Confucianism, Zhuangzi saw so many Confucian scholars dressed in Confucian clothing. They wore circular hats, representing understanding of astronomical knowledge; they wore square clogs, representing geographical knowledge; they wore jade pieces, representing an ability to make decisions.

However, Zhuangzi thought all of that finery was utterly specious. No one really likes things which are opposed to human nature such as benevolence, justice, propriety and wisdom. Confucian scholars' purpose he believed was to flatter the kings

Zhuangzi giving tests to pseudo scholars.

and win fame.

To test his idea, he and the king of the Lu State made a bet. A decree was promulgated: Any unqualified Confucian scholars would suffer the death penalty.

As a result, a dramatic scene ensued. At dusk that day, nearly all Confucian scholars and clothes disappeared completely, a scene quite different from that morning.

But Zhuangzi did not know that although this ruse made many people take off their Confucian clothes, the social reality of deceiving people and usurping state power through the beautiful masks of "rites and music" remained unchanged. His idea of suggesting that feudal princes abdicate seemed somewhat absurd at that time.

煎桂可食故伐之漆可用故割之皆知有

用之用不知無用之用也

莊子內篇第六 大宗師

古之真人其寢不夢 深云無意想也 其覺無憂 注云當所遇而安也

涸魚相與處於陸相呴以濕相濡以沫不如相忘於江湖

夫大塊載我以形勞我以生佚我以老息我以死 藏舟於壑

藏山於澤夜半有力者負而走昧者不知 注云方

Hun Dun:
Highest Realm of Idealism

What constitutes the utopia in the eyes of Zhuangzi? The answer is very simple: No king. If a king is required, he should be like Hun Dun as depicted by Zhuangzi.

Both the Confucian School and Zhuangzi advocated idealism, but they are quite different in essence.

Confucius aimed to build up the social and political order through cultural concepts. He emphasized the role of music and harmony in preserving order, and desired a harmonious and orderly society. But Zhuangzi noticed the negative effects of civilization, and thought that rites and music in fact restrained people. So he emphasized human freedom because he thought that all systems and standards were limited. However, the Confucian School thought that systems and standards were paramount, so Zhuangzi refuted the ideas of the Confucian School. He insisted that

A bird's eye view of the Imperial Palace of the Ming (1368-1644) and Qing (1644-1911) Dynasties. A total of 24 emperors once lived here.

Taoist Holy Land of Nanyue Hengshan Mountain.

these systems and standards are temporary and limited in history.

Confucius provided rulers with a complete political theory from the perspective of human society, while Zhuangzi focused on the liberation of the human mind from the perspective of nature. After hundreds of years of collision, the result finally emerged in the first century BC: Confucianism was highly respected, while Zhuangzi's philosophy only really spread among the common people.

煎桂可食故伐之漆可用故割之皆知有用之用不知無用之用也

莊子內篇第六 大宗師

古之真人其寢不夢 注云無意想也 其覺無憂 注云當所遇而安也 泉涸魚相與處於陸相呴以濕相濡以沫不如相忘於江湖

夫大塊載我以形勞我以生佚我以老息我以死也 藏舟於壑藏山於澤夜半有力者而走之昧者不知 注云

'Zhuangzi': A Critical Book

On February 21, 1677, Spinoza passed away quietly at home. People found a sentence in his finished book *Ethics*: The free man seldom thinks of death. His intelligence is about life rather than death.

Through the ages, life and death is an eternal human topic. What were Zhuangzi's view on death?

He first encountered death when his wife died. After hearing the news, his friend Hui Shi came to offer his condolences. But what Hui Shi saw in Zhuangzi's home really shocked him.

Zhuangzi was sitting on the ground, singing and beating an earthenware basin between his legs like a drum with one

Zhuangzi thought people should treat life and death calmly.

wooden stick.

Hui Shi rebuked him: “Your wife gave birth to and raised your children for you. Now she has died. You should cry instead of singing? How can you behave like this?”

Zhuangzi answered: No one could be more sorrowful than me. But I think birth, senility, illness and death are the natural law. Now she has returned to nature where she can rest quietly. I should not cry and bother her with my tears. Life and death are just natural phenomena.

Zhuangzi thought people should treat life and death calmly. People originate from and eventually return to nature - a process of metempsychosis. It should be natural and quiet like a seasonal change.

At his wife's funeral, Zhuangzi did not respond to other people's rebukes. He still sang his songs while beating away on the basin. The clouds above his head kept changing. He seemed to see his dead wife fly up to the sky slowly, and then gradually merge with the clouds, sunlight and the air surrounding Zhuangzi.

Shortly afterwards, his best friend Hui Shi also passed away. Zhuangzi and Hui Shi had been "rivals" in terms of philosophy for their whole lives. Their topics had included whether fish were happy, and whether a large gourd was useful. Zhuangzi told a thought-provoking parable to offer condolence to his friend. Finally, he sighed with emotion: I've lost my debating rival forever!

How would he face his own death?

Before the death of Zhuangzi, many of his disciples expressed the intention of holding an elaborate funeral for him.

Zhuangzi said: "It is enough to be accompanied by heaven and earth, sun and moon, stars and all things on earth. What need is there for a grand funeral!"

One disciple said: "I am afraid the crows will eat you!"

Zhuangzi said: "Both crows and ants may eat me. But if you favor ants, surely that is unfair, isn't it?"

From his outlook on birth and death we can see the ultimate significance of his life philosophy which advocated remaining aloof from the world. Zhuangzi's feeling about life reflects a larger sense of time-space beyond the imagination of ordinary

The tomb of Zhuangzi.

people. That is to say, Zhuangzi thought that each person exists in ethical relationships, and in nature. Since I am a person in nature, I should live based on the larger values and end my life finally. The funerary objects are required only for "principles" in the secular world, which is just what Zhuangzi wanted to overcome.

Zhuangzi had a famous saying choose living in mud rather than commiting suicide. This saying eventually evolved into a popular sentence about universal philosophy: "To live is better than to die." Of course, the connotation of Zhuangzi's thought far surpasses the general understanding of life and death.

He always stressed cherishing life, but he was not afraid of death. He said: "Nature endows me with a body, makes me fatigued through life, lets me get old through time, and makes me rest forever through death;

Zhuang Zhou's Dreaming of Becoming a Butterfly (copy), water-and-ink on silk by Liu Guandao (painter), Yuan Dynasty.

nature is changeable, and people must follow the natural laws, to treat everything calmly."

Life originates from nature, and will return to nature. Zhuangzi advocated freedom at all times. Zhuangzi's romantic and unrestrained words like those of a poet annotate life and death perfectly. He became eternal in nature.

Zhuangzi's understanding of the nature of life is unique. For thousands of years,

"Zhuangzi's understanding of life and death" has basically become general: What is the source of life? How will life end ultimately? Life is born when the Qi (pneuma) gathers, and life ends when the Qi is dispersed. Qi returns to the original place where it was formed. This is the "Dahua" concept of Zhuangzi. All of us are cultivated through "Dahua". We are born and die in a way that satisfies natural law.

煎桂可食故伐之漆可用故割之皆知有用之用不知無用之用也

莊子內篇第六 大宗師

古之真人其寢不夢（注云無意想也）其覺無憂（注云當所遇而安也）

涸魚相與處於陸相呴以濕相濡以沫不如相忘於江湖

大塊載我以形勞我以生佚我以老息我以死也 藏舟於壑

藏山於澤夜半有力者負而走昧者不知注云方

The Oriental Great Master's Keen Insight into Life

Zhuangzi held an open, naturalistic attitude towards life, which, from ancient times to today, has exerted a profound influence on Chinese people and thought.

Clear evidence of this can be seen in the fact that in the 1970s, a great man of China said: "You can hold a celebration after my death. Mao Zedong may die, but his dialectics will be victorious!

Mao Zedong's open philosophy on life reflects the historical elements of Zhuangzi's thought to some extent.

Even today, ordinary Chinese people have two happy things in life: Marriage and the delivery of children. Marriage and the birth of children are the start of life,

Portrait of Zhuangzi.

and represent red and happy affairs, while ageing, sickness and death are the end of life, and constitute some sad but still happy affairs.

These red and white happy affairs represent two ends of life, and birth and death are just a conversion of one's life status. Feeling easy and optimistic about birth and death, Chinese perhaps have inherited Zhuangzi's view of life and death.

As Wen Yiduo, a famous modern Chinese thinker, said Zhuangzi is in the blood of

Chinese culture.

Zhuangzi was a philosopher with a distinctive personality in the Chinese history of thought. In his eyes, bigness and smallness, life and death, rightness and wrongness, kindness and evil, and usefulness and uselessness-all these concepts are relative, but they don't absolutely constitute the opposite of one another, but can rather change their positions, depending on the angles of perception.

Zhuangzi offered a very vivid example: We only need a ground area equal to the size of two feet, but if you cut off the ground outside the ground where your feet stand to a very large depth, then, can you still stand firmly? Can you still walk?

With this example, Zhuangzi made one thing clear: Certain things are useless for a concrete practical purpose, but this does

Wedding and funeral parties.

not mean it makes no sense. Zhuangzi said, "a thing serving no concrete purpose is a thing serving a general purposes".

In Chinese cultural history, Zhuangzi brought romance to literature: His fables quote a diversity of stories. They give us interesting scenes. They use language freely with rich imagination, and they create unusual and pleasant experiences for readers. Even today, folk artists in the hometown of Zhuangzi are still fascinated by the picturesque dreams of the great thinker.

In the hometown of the master, people believe a person with an outstanding forehead usually thinks on a broader canvas and thinks more than others. For this reason, when portraying Zhuangzi, folk artists prefer to give a prominent, outstanding forehead to the master. This image is both based on people's impressions on Zhuangzi as recorded in literature, and also takes into consideration the character of the thinker. The artists believe this image can accurately express the feelings and essence of Zhuangzi's dream of a butterfly.

In traditional Chinese culture, Zhuangzi's dream of a butterfly is a very famous story, while in another Chinese traditional literary works *Liang Shanbo and Zhu Yingtai*, the love story between Liang Shanbo and Zhu Yingtai climaxes when they change into butterflies: The hero and the heroine change into butterflies in order to follow love at the cost of their lives.

Changing into butterflies represents a conversion from one form of existence to another form, and such a concept of conversion comes from Zhuangzi. The change to butterflies also comes from Zhuangzi's stories, while the freedom and simultaneous dancing after the change into

Liang Shanbo and Zhu Yingtai, lovers, turned into butterflies upon their death.

butterflies also originate from the great thinker. Zhuangzi also left his mark on Chinese literature. For example, Chinese poetry stresses imagination, Chinese painting pays attention to blank spaces, and expression pursues infinite meanings with finite languages.

Cao Xueqin, the author of *A Dream of Red Mansions*, expressed the view through Miaoyu, a character in the novel that Zhuangzi wrote better than other Chinese sages in ancient times. Lu Xun, a renowned Chinese writer in modern times, noted that Zhuangzi's articles were free and diverse, and exceeded the writing of all the great authors in the Pre-Qin Period.

At the core of Zhuangzi's philosophy are Xiao and Yao, where Xiao represents liberation from any restriction, and Yao means being boundless and infinite.

If we describe Zhuangzi's lifestyle in only

one word, it must be "Xiao". In his life, Zhuangzi followed his own path, and never restrained himself with secular standards. His manner of thinking manner can be described using one character, that is, "Yao". He imagined the worlds above and under the ground, and extended his thought to every possible point, regardless of space and time. If we describe the paramount realm Zhuangzi pursued in life, it must be "Xiao" and "Yao".

In reality, Zhuangzi attempted to play a role as a spiritual saviour of the Chinese. In his eyes, freedom is the most fundamental spiritual pursuit in life. He revealed the truth behind the lifestyles of numerous people in a profound and aesthetic fashion. Therefore, Zhuangzi's unique thoughts about life have influenced Chinese culture and lifestyles to a large extent. For more than two thousand years, if there had been

Water-ink Chinese painting Lotus Flower by Bada Shanren of the Qing Dynasty. White Space of the painting is held even today as a good idea in painting creation.

no Zhuangzi, the Chinese people would have a much tighter mental realm and a much narrower mind.

In the modern dictionary, "Xiao" and

Chinese characters reading "Xiao Yao", meaning "free and easy".

"Yao" are associated with a free and worry-free life based on a good material foundation. However, while enjoying the pleasure created by material civilization, people have to tolerate the pain that lies behind such pleasure.

The conflict between humans and nature keeps intensifying, as evidenced by ecosystem imbalances and environmental pollution; the conflict between humans and society keeps escalating, as evidenced by the determined pursuit of monetary wealth and enjoyment; and the human spiritual crisis is intensifying, as evidenced by the distortions of personality and pessimism. In the face of so many confusions, how can people become free and mentally unrestricted?

One scholar gave a vivid example to compare oriental and western cultures: An American accused a kindergarten because the teachers in the kindergarten were teaching his child to recognize letters. He justified his accusation by saying the teachers' instruction would restrict his child's imagination. For example, when the teachers teach his child the letter "O", the teachers will definitively tell the child this letter is "O". Then, how can the child imagine the letter to be a peach or apple? Is this acceptable? However, the teachers specify this letter must be "O", so the child's imagination will be blocked by the teachers. In reality, this is a conflict, because every person must experience the

The world enjoys free life and happiness.

process of socialization, but the question is: Must the child be fully restricted by these codes? That is to say, we must pursue the socialization of humans, but we must also have the awareness that it can be acceptable to break existing codes. That is to say, there must be something that is bigger than the code in the world. Then, what could be such a thing? Zhuangzi, who lived 2,300 years ago, answered this question: Such a thing does exist - it is freedom.

In the Chinese history of philosophy, Zhuangzi and Lao Tzu, the founders of Taoism, are always put together and collectively known as "Lao Tzu and Zhuangzi". Their philosophic thought system is called the "Philosophy of Lao Tzu and Zhuangzi" in academic circles. The representative works of Zhuangzi, include the classical articles of *Enjoyment of life in Untroubled Ease* and *the On Leveling All Things*. The essence of Zhuangzi's thought relies on "harmony between man and nature" and "quiescence and inaction". His doctrines cover all aspects of social life in ancient China, but were eventually attributed to Lao Tzu's philosophical thought in terms of spirit. Therefore, Zhuangzi and Lao Tzu are inseparable in Taoist philosophy.

The place where Zhuangzi passed away is a mystery. Different people have different opinions. So far, no one can accurately decide the specific location. However, people in those places called the hometowns of Zhuangzi, have built plain and unvarnished tombs made of loess for him. No imperial handwriting can be found on the inscriptions of his tombs. Only the signatures of numerous common people remain. Maybe people know nothing about what's buried in the tomb. There is also no information about his descendants. But people there believe that leisurely Zhuangzi still walks alongside them.

Zhuangzi can be seen as a mythical character spanning back thousands of years. According to legend, he ultimately changed into a butterfly. Perhaps he really did become a butterfly ....

Mausoleum of Zhuangzi.

自煎桂可食故伐之漆可用故割之皆知有

用之用不知無用之用也

莊子內篇第六 大宗師

古之真人其寢不夢 注云無意想也 其覺無憂 注云當所遇而安也 泉

涸魚相與處於陸相呴以濕相濡以沫不相忘於江湖

夫大塊載我以形勞我以生佚我以老息我以死也 藏舟於壑

藏山於澤夜半有力者而走昧者不知 注云

Quotations from Zhuangzi

Unknowable 'Tao' and the World

☆

Floating clouds and dust like wild horses galloping, result from the mutual influence of a biological breath. Is the deep blue of the sky its natural color? Is the sky really boundless?

☆

One-sided cognition will hinder the pursuit of truth, and sweet words will become barriers of real language.

☆

"This" and "that" can be converted mutually. They both have two sides, namely "yes" and "no".

☆

Nature and mankind coexist and unite into the whole.

☆

I feel confused about the strong desire to be alive. I hate death just as though I was reluctant to go home during my childhood.

☆

Zhuangzi dreamed about becoming a butterfly dancing happily. He did think he was a butterfly. After waking up, he was surprised to find he was still himself. He wondered whether he became a butterfly or whether the butterfly became him. After all, Zhuangzi and the butterfly are different. The change of object and self is called "materialization".

☆

Things are different from each other.

For example, in the human body the liver and gall bladder are very close to each other, but they are just like two countries that exist far from each other. All things have similarities. From this perspective, everything is the same.

☆

Nobody can find his shadow in the flowing water but only in static water; many other things can be static, too.

☆

People record the truth through written words. In fact, what's recorded is only human language. Language indeed is valuable for its significance in communicating ideas – by itself it is nothing. However, words are recorded and handed down because people value languages.

☆

Heaven and Earth have the greatest virtues, seasons have clear rules, and all things have an inherent truth, but they keep silent instead of showing off. Saints understood the truth of all things by studying the virtues of heaven and earth.

☆

People understand knowledge and truth by learning, practicing and discussing what is strange to them. Mankind's cognition stops in the face of things that are strange to him.

☆

Mankind may throw away the bamboo cage after fishing with it; mankind may throw away the rabbit mesh after catching the rabbit with it; mankind may forget a language after expressing ideas with it.

☆

A chi-long whip can be half-cut forever.

Life Ideology of Inaction and Reclusiveness

☆

There are certain people in the whole world who will not work harder no matter how much people praise them, nor become more depressed if criticized.

☆

A truly extraordinary person with the highest accomplishments can forget himself, think not of merits, fame or wealth.

☆

Trees on mountains are cut down because they can be made into timber; oil is burned because it can be ignited and illuminate other things. The cherry bay tree is cut down because its bark can be eaten; the lacquer tree is cut down because its juice can be used. All people know the meaning of "useful", but do not know the meaning of "useless".

☆

Each ox or horse has four legs, which is natural; a horse is bridled, and an ox is reeved in the nose, which is a man-made device for hobbling them for greater control. Therefore, natural laws should not be destroyed by human laws. The inherent laws should not be broken artificially. Fame should not be pursued at the cost of sacrificing natural instincts.

☆

The greatest joy is to be free from the so-called worldly joy, and the highest honor is to get rid of the so-called worldly honor.

☆

Straight trees will be cut down first, and wells with sweet water will dry first.

☆

One man was afraid of his own shadow and hated his own footprint. He ran fast to get rid of them. But the more he raised his legs, the more footprints he left; the faster he ran, the closer the shadow approached him. He thought it is because he ran slowly, so he continuously accelerated the pace. As a result, he was so exhausted that he died. He did not know the shadow would disappear in the darkness, and the footprints would disappear when he stopped.

Mankind's Natural Instincts and Moral Cultivation

☆

Far-sighted people are broad-minded and tolerant, while shortsighted people haggle over every ounce. Smart remarks seem to be plain, while gossip is tedious.

☆

Moral corruption results from pursuit of fame, and wisdom exposure results from desire to excel over others. Fame is the reason of struggle, while wisdom is the means of struggle. Both are sources of misfortune or disaster. We should not only focus on fame and wisdom.

☆

A bright mirror has no dust, and a dusty mirror is not bright. People will not make mistakes if they often stay together with virtuous people.

☆

Physical deficiencies of a person of high morality will be ignored.

☆

Nature and wisdom of a man with too many hobbies and desires will be obscured or fade away.

☆

Extraordinary people live in harmony with nature rather than the secular world.

☆

Like a mirror, the saint's heart can reflect the true world. He never drives away, caters to or hides anything. Therefore, he is free from hurt.

☆

A wild duck's legs are short. But if we make its legs long forcibly, it will feel pain. A crane's legs are long. But if we make its legs short forcibly, it will become sad.

☆

Little confusion will make people lose their direction, and large confusion will make people lose their nature.

☆

When water is static, people's faces can be clearly seen. Even and straight features of water are in line with the level measurement standard. Clever craftsmen thus made a leveling instrument. Static water is clear, letting alone the quiet mind of a saint. A Saint's heart can mirror nature.

☆

The fisherman is brave to walk in the water without fear of flood dragon; the hunter is brave to walk on land without fear of rhinos, tigers and other wild beasts. The martyr is brave to treat death as usual as survival. Fates are different. The saint is brave to face dangers and disasters.

☆

People forget the feet because of comfortable shoes or forget the waists because of comfortable waistbands.

☆

Dogs only good at crying are not called "good dogs", and people only good at speaking are not called "virtuous people".

☆

Pursuing a noble reputation by beautifying some shallow theories, you will stay far away from the great wisdom.

☆

Nobody is willing to approach a man intolerant to others; a man without intimate friends feels strange towards others.

☆

A person who likes to praise others face to face also likes making malicious remarks behind their back.

Society and Politics

☆

Even if the chef refuses to cook at the time of sacrifice, the emcee will not replace the chef to cook.

☆

Ordinary people risk their lives for wealth, scholars risk their lives for fame, officials risk their lives for territory, and saints risk their lives for happiness of the world. Such people are different in terms of career and fame, but are the same in harming nature and risking lives for what they want.

☆

Craftsmen are sinful for destroying the complete timber to make appliances; saints are sinful for destroying morality to advocate kindheartedness and justice.

☆

Even If there are saints, robbers will not stop their disruptive behavior.

☆

Some thieves are executed, while people

stealing State power become vassals or kings.

☆

During the reign of wise Emperor Yaodi, people were so ecstatic and joyous that they became restless; during the reign of cruel Emperor Jie of Xia Dynasty, people felt so worried and painful that they became sad. Restless and sad moods are not the normal form of life. The forms against natural rules cannot exist for a long time.

☆

Elegant music is not appreciated by secular people who like popular folk songs. Therefore, profound remarks are not accepted by secular people, and words of wisdom are have little significance for them. It is because secular words dominate.

☆

People with shared benefits are likely to abandon each other in case of poverty, disaster and distress.

☆

Friendship among gentlemen is light like water; friendship among villains is sweet like wine. Gentlemen are close to each other despite light friendship; villains are separated from each other despite sweet friendship.

☆

Powerful emperors are not necessarily noble; poor ordinary people are not necessarily humble. The difference between noble and humble people is good or bad behavior.

☆

Skilled people are more painstaking, and

wise people are more worried. Like the floating boat, people without talent have no pursuit, and drift everywhere.

Philosophy About the World and Life

☆

Shallow water cannot support large ships.

☆

Little insects with a life of only one day do not know the concept of "month"; cicadas with a life of one season do not know the concept of "spring and autumn".

☆

The wren makes its nest in the deep forest, but it only occupies one branch. The shrewmouse only drinks enough water at the riverside.

☆

Our life is limited, but knowledge is unlimited. Pursuit of infinite knowledge in the limited life makes people very tired.

☆

The firewood will be burned out in time, but kindling material can be kept for ever.

☆

It is very easy to keep static, so as not to leave traces; it is very difficult to walk without traces.

☆

It is easy to do at the beginning, but complex and difficult at the end.

☆

Have never heard a story about the

mantis? It raised its claws to block the moving wheel. It's so arrogant that it did not know it is too weak to do that.

☆

If one loves a person or a thing in a subjective way, the loved one may be hurt. So, we should be prudent in treating people or things.

☆

For lack of water, fish were trapped on the land. They helped each other, mutually blew the air and wetted each other with saliva. But they were more willing to live freely in the lake instead of through mutual care.

☆

Nature gives birth to me, life makes me hard, aging makes me leisurely, and death makes me rest.

☆

In order to guard against thieves, people certainly will tighten the knots and reinforce locks, which is so-called "wisdom". But robbers will run away after picking up boxes and bags, while worrying about whether they are solid. If so, the previous "wisdom" means collection of wealth for robbers.

☆

More boys mean more worries; more properties mean more troubles; longer life means more distress.

☆

Three people walk together. If one loses the direction, they can still reach the destination because the minority is confused; if two of them lose the direction, they cannot reach the destination because the majority are confused.

☆

Due to space limit, frogs in the well cannot see the sea; due to time limit, insects that only live in the summer cannot enjoy the snow and ice; due to education limit, short-sighted people have no idea about general principles.

☆

Significant things cannot be observed fully from the tiny perspective; tiny things cannot be observed clearly from a significant perspective.

☆

A small bag cannot contain a large object, and water in a deep well cannot be fetched with a short rope.

☆

The most serious tragedy is death of the soul rather than the body.

☆

Life is so transient, just as though a horse gallops past the wall gap.

☆

Nature makes me pleased and happy! But sadness follows the happiness so soon. I cannot resist the arrival or departure of any sorrow and joy. Sadly, people's inner world is only the inn of external things.

☆

People will certainly laugh at a man who shoots a flying bird with precious pearls, because what he desires for is cheaper than what he consumes.

☆

People's minds are more dangerous than high mountains and rapids, and are more difficult to understand than nature. The natural world has its rules, but people's minds hidden behind the appearance are very unpredictable.

图书在版编目（CIP）数据

天地逍遥游——庄子：英文/徐远翔，印永健著；王壹晨，王国振译．
—北京：五洲传播出版社，2014.6
（中国智慧）
ISBN 978-7-5085-2766-6

Ⅰ．①天… Ⅱ．①徐… ②印… ③王… ④王… Ⅲ．①庄周（约前369～前286）-传记-英文 Ⅳ．①B223.5

中国版本图书馆CIP数据核字(2014)第111269号

顾　　问：冷成金
作　　者：徐远翔　印永健
译　　者：王壹晨　王国振
封面绘画：郑玉阗
插图作者：王振国
图片提供：CFP　东方IC　五洲传播　紫航文化
出 版 人：荆孝敏
责任编辑：王　莉　韩　旭
特约编辑：王　峰
设计总监：蔡　程
设计制作：邹　红

天地逍遥游——庄子

出版发行：五洲传播出版社
地　　址：北京市海淀区北三环中路31号生产力大楼B座7层（100088）
电　　话：010-82005927，010-82007837（发行部）
网　　址：www.cicc.org.cn
开　　本：32开
印　　张：4.625
设计承制：北京紫航文化艺术有限公司
印　　刷：北京盛天行健艺术印刷有限公司
版　　次：2014年6月第一版　2014年6月第一次印刷
书　　号：ISBN 978-7-5085-2766-6
定　　价：53.00元